"THE ONLY

LIGHT

IN THE DARKNESS

IS

HEROISM."

—EDITH HAMILTON

HEIMDALL

THOUGHT

BURI

MEMORY

FREKI

ODIN

FRIGG

GERI

SIF

THOR

FREYA

MAGNI

BALDER

NANNA

HOD

FAVORITE NORSE MYTHS

RETOLD BY MARY POPE OSBORNE
ILLUSTRATED BY TROY HOWELL

SCHOLASTIC INC.
New York Toronto London Auckland Sydney

BRAGI

IDUN

TYR

HERMOD

NJORD

MIMIR

SIGYN

SKADI

LOKI

MIDGARD
SERPENT

To NATHANIEL —M.P.O.   To OLIN —T.H.

WITH SPECIAL THANKS TO DIANNE HESS —M.P.O. AND T.H.

The quotes at the beginnings of chapters 3, 4, 9, and 14 are from the *Poetic Edda*,
translated by Henry Adams Bellows.
Reprinted by courtesy of the American-Scandinavian Foundation.

Special thanks to David Yerkes for fact-checking the manuscript.

ISBN 0-590-48047-2

Text copyright © 1996 by Mary Pope Osborne. Illustrations copyright © 1996 by Troy Howell.
All rights reserved. Published by Scholastic Inc.

12 11 10 9 8 7 6 5 4 3   2   7 8 9/9 0 1 2/0
Printed in the U.S.A.   08

The display type was set in Sophia by Carter & Cone Type.
The text type was set in Jensen by NK Graphics, Keene, NH.

Design by Marijka Kostiw.

Troy Howell's art was rendered on rag board in acrylics with oil washes.

TABLE OF CONTENTS

INTRODUCTION

LONG AGO, THE WORLD WAS MADE OF ICE AND MIST AND FLAME. Out of these vapors swirled an evil frost-giant and a great ice cow. The cow licked the snow until she licked a god into being. The god's grandsons murdered the frost-giant and then made nine worlds from his huge body.

This is the way the universe began, according to the creation story of old Norway, first told over a thousand years ago. The nine worlds of this universe were filled with gods, goddesses, giants, dwarves, and elves — many of whom you will meet in this book.

The Norse gods and goddesses were not considered to be fanciful characters by the people of old Norway. They were the deities of a living religion. People told sacred stories about them. They offered sacrifices to them and prayed to wooden images of them.

In the year 840, the seafaring men of Norway, called Vikings, escaped a ruthless king and crossed the ocean to the island of Iceland. For over a century, they practiced their pagan rituals and orally passed down the sacred stories and poems about their gods and goddesses. The stories told about the battles between the gods and the giants. They explained what caused thunder, lightning, and the changing of seasons.

But in the year 1000, all of Iceland adopted the religion of Christianity. Thereafter, the gods and goddesses of the old religion were replaced by the God of Christianity; and the stories of the pagan Norse religion were replaced by the sacred stories of the Christian Bible.

Before all the old stories faded away, a collection called the *Poetic Edda* was gathered together. No one knows who the author was, or even if there was more than one author. Later, in the thirteenth century, an Icelandic chieftain named Snorri Sturluson also told a number of old stories in a book called the *Prose Edda.*

The *Poetic Edda* and the *Prose Edda* are our primary sources for the pre-Christian stories of old Norway. Today we call these stories *myths,* for people no longer believe them to be literally true.

The Norse myths often depict a strange, bleak world, a world inhabited by warring giants and gods, a world heading toward its own destruction. This sort of world is not surprising when we consider that long ago, the people of Iceland lived short, harsh lives filled with darkness and loneliness. Families endured long winters in isolated farmhouses a day's ride from one another. They struggled against blizzards, ice storms, and scarcity of food.

What is surprising is that, given such rugged living conditions, the people of Iceland still celebrated humor, wisdom, friendship, and most of all, heroism.

They celebrated a heroism confined not only to the battlefield. The god, Odin, endured torture to learn the magic symbols for writing. The Norse storytellers believed a poet was as much a hero as a warrior. The poet had the magic power to name things; he was the carrier of memory and history.

The hammer that belongs to the hero Thor is not so much a weapon of violence as a weapon used to order the universe. The giants impersonate the chaotic, brutal forces of nature; and when Thor slays them, he is making it possible for human life to prevail.

In the Norse stories, the gods control the giants in two ways: They either slay them or marry them. This marriage of good and evil is further demonstrated in the character Loki, a relative of both the gods and the giants. Loki offers paradox as he demonstrates that evil can reside in good; and good, in evil.

While the goddesses are not main figures in the surviving Norse stories, the *Prose Edda* states that the goddesses were no less important than the gods, and we see evidence of this in such powerful female characters as the Valkyries, the Norns, and Odin's wife, Frigg. Perhaps it's possible that stories about the goddesses simply did not survive from olden times.

Though the Norse myths spring from the early Viking people, they have many ideas in common with the myths of other lands. The mischief-maker, Loki, joins the shape-shifting tricksters of Native American myth and traditional African stories. Balder's descent to the land of the dead is not unlike that of the Egyptian god Osiris or the Babylonian god Tammuz. Thor reminds us of Indra and Zeus, the thunder gods of India and Greece. And the end of the old Norse world, called Ragnarok, reflects all the great deluges that have ended one age so that another might begin, such as the flood in the Judeo-Christian Bible or the Anasazi diaspora of the Navajo folklore.

I believe that, like all the great stories of the world, the Norse myths belong to *all* of us: to the people of Scandinavia, to the people of every culture around the world, to you and me. All people of all times have experienced the same fears, longings, and sorrows of the Norse gods and goddesses. All of us can rejoice in their courage, strength, and humor.

In these retellings, I have tried to present the stories as simply and clearly as possible, without sacrificing their mythic tone; and to bring out the humor and irony that the old poets hinted at in their spare tellings. To help bridge the distance between the old and the new, each chapter begins with a quote from the *Poetic Edda,* written in the tenth century.

Most of all, I sought to make the stories as compelling and magical as they were a thousand years ago, when told in that rugged, icy land, in a lonely farmhouse . . . by the hearth . . . close to the light.

CREATION: THE NINE WORLDS

Twas the earliest of times
When Ymir lived;
There was no sand nor sea
Nor cooling wave.
Earth had not been,
Nor Heaven on high,
There was a yawning void
And grass no where.

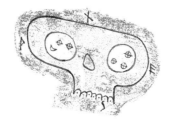

IN THE MORNING OF TIME THERE WAS NO SAND, no sea, and no clouds. There was no heaven, no earth, and no grass. There was only a region of icy mist called Niflheim, a region of fire called Muspell, and a great yawning empty void between them called Ginnungagap.

Over time, the flames of Muspell warmed the frozen vapors of Niflheim, and ice melted into water and began to drip. Quickened with life, the water dripped into the void and formed into two gigantic creatures.

The first was a wicked frost-giant named Ymir. The second was a huge cow named Audumla. As Ymir drank Audumla's milk, he grew bigger and stronger. One night as Ymir slept, a troll with six heads

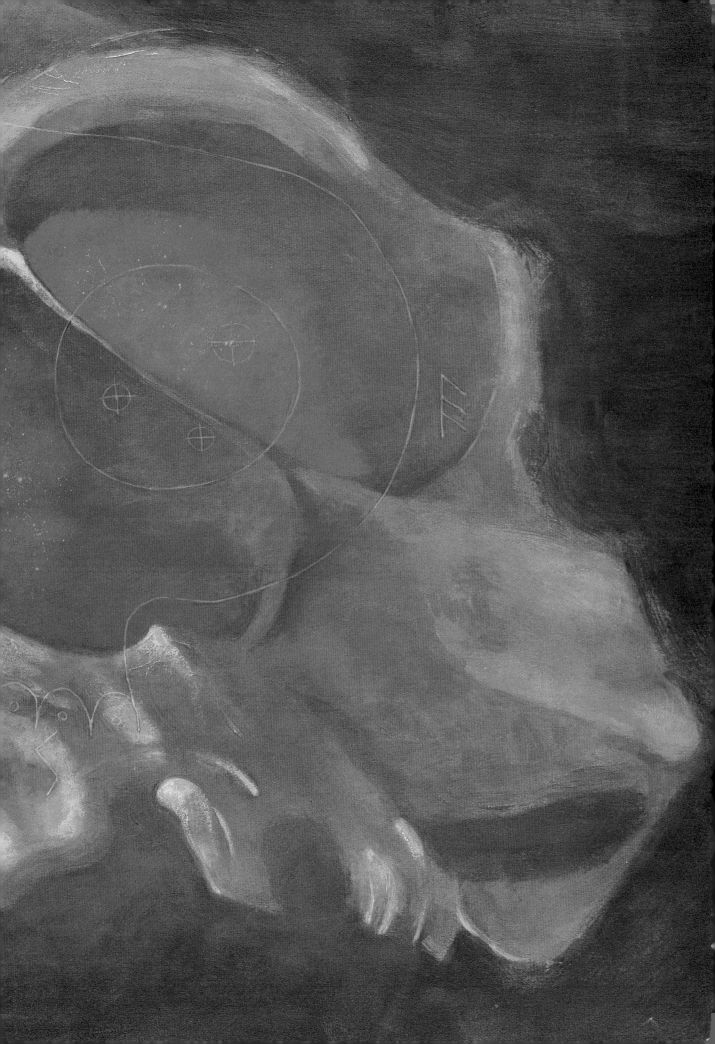

grew from the soles of his feet, and a male and a female frost-giant sprung from Ymir's warm armpit.

The ice cow also brought about life. As she licked salty ice blocks, she slowly licked a new creature into being. The first day hair came forth; on the second day came a head — and finally, on the third day, the body of a new giant emerged. This giant was a good giant whose name was Buri. His sons and grandsons became gods instead of giants, and they stood for all that was good and honorable.

The greatest of Buri's grandsons was the god Odin. Odin led his brothers against the wicked frost-giant Ymir. They killed Ymir, and ever after that time, the gods and giants were deadly enemies.

After Odin and his brothers had slain the frost-giant, they dragged his enormous body into the void. Ymir's flesh became the earth. His blood became the sea. His bones became mountains; his hair, trees; and his teeth, stones.

Then Odin and his brothers discovered worms living in the earth that was Ymir's flesh, and they turned them into dwarves and dark elves and sent them to mine the ore beneath the mountains and hills. The world of the dwarves was called Nidavellir; and the world of the dark elves was called Svartalfheim.

The gods also discovered lovely creatures in the soil. They called them light elves and placed them in a world called Alfheim.

The blood that flowed from Ymir's veins became the sea, and it drowned all the frost-giants. Only two escaped in a boat and began a new race of giants. From this race came all warlocks, enchanters, ogres, and witches, including a witch in the woods who gave birth to all the wolves of the world.

Then Odin set Ymir's skull over the earth and called it the sky. He spread the giant's brains throughout the sky and called them clouds. At the four corners of the sky, he placed four dwarves named Nordri, Sudri, Austri, and Vestri — or North, South, East, and West.

Odin and his brothers caught sparks from the fires of Muspell and turned them into stars. They put a girl named Sun and a boy named Moon into two chariots of fire and placed them in the sky. From then on, Sun and Moon were continuously chased by a ferocious wolf named Moon-Hound.

Odin also gave chariots to a goddess named Night and her son Day. Night rode behind a horse called Frosty-Mane; the foam from his mouth became the dew of early morning.

Then Odin and his kin took Ymir's eyebrows and turned them into a land called Midgard. They made two humans from trees — a man from an ash and a woman from an elm. They gave the humans spirit, life, speech, hearing, sight, clothing, temples, and shrines.

Then the gods left their human friends in Midgard and crossed over a flaming rainbow bridge to a world called Asgard. There, they built golden halls — one for the gods and one for the goddesses, for the goddesses were no less important than the gods.

Odin, the greatest of the gods, was the god of War and Death. After a battle ended, warrior maidens called Valkyries, picked up the dead and carried them to Odin's palace, Valhalla, Hall of the Slain.

Odin's wife, Frigg, sat on the throne next to him. She was the goddess of knowledge and knew all that happened in the worlds. Frigg could look into the future and see the fates of gods and men, but she kept all her visions a secret, never sharing them with anyone.

Odin had many sons. With Frigg, he had twin boys, Balder and Hod. Balder, their favorite, was like the sun. He was the most gentle and beautiful of all the gods. Hod was blind and ruled the black hours of night.

Odin's second favorite son was Thor. The strongest of all the gods, Thor was the god of the sky and thunder. His wife, Sif, had long hair made of gold.

The god Heimdall was also a son of Odin. Night and day, he

watched the rainbow bridge, keeping out enemies. His sight was so keen, he could see in the dark; his sense of sound was so sharp, he could hear wool growing on sheep.

In the early days, there were two kinds of gods: the Aesir and the Vanir. Odin and his kin were Aesir and lived in Asgard. The Vanir, the gods of nature, lived in Vanaheim.

One day the Aesir and Vanir went to war. The fighting lasted until both grew weary and decided to become friends. Thereafter, the Vanir god Njord lived in Asgard and ruled the wind and seas. His son, Frey, ruled the rain and sunshine. And his daughter, Freya, was the goddess of love.

There was one god who was neither Aesir nor Vanir. His name was Loki, and he was the son of two giants and the foster-brother of Odin. Loki was the most dangerous of all the gods, for sometimes he was a friend and sometimes he was purely evil. No one ever knew when he could be trusted.

From the mighty halls of Asgard, the gods and goddesses ruled all the nine worlds. They were:

> *Niflheim,* world of mist and the dead
> *Muspell,* world of fire
> *Midgard,* world of humans
> *Jotunheim,* world of frost-giants
> *Alfheim,* world of light elves
> *Nidavellir,* world of the dwarves
> *Svartalfheim,* world of the dark elves
> *Vanaheim,* world of the Vanir gods
> *Asgard,* world of the Aesir gods and goddesses

Above all these worlds was a wondrous tree called Yggdrasil, or the World Tree. A wise eagle sat on top of the tree, surveying the universe.

One of the tree's roots grew into Niflheim where a dreadful serpent ceaselessly gnawed on the root. A busy squirrel named Ratatosk scurried up and down the World Tree, carrying insults back and forth between the serpent and the eagle.

Another root of the tree grew into Asgard. Under that root was Urd's Well, whose pure waters helped protect the World Tree, for it suffered terribly from deer and goats eating its leaves.

A third root coiled into Jotunheim. And under that root was Mimir's Well, whose magic waters held all the wisdom and memory of ancient lore.

Hidden in Mimir's Well was a trumpet that belonged to Heimdall, the guardian of Asgard. All the gods knew that one day a blast on Heimdall's trumpet would announce the last bitter battle between the gods and the forces of evil. This final battle, called Ragnarok, would bring about the total destruction of the nine worlds.

ODIN'S THREE QUESTS

I trust I hung
On that windy tree,
Nine whole days and nights.
Stabbed with a spear,
None refreshed me e're,
With food nor drink.
I peered right down into the deep;
Crying aloud I lifted the runes,
Then back I fell from there.

I. THE QUEST FOR WISDOM

EARLY EVERY MORNING, ODIN, the father of all the gods, sat on his throne in a golden hall of Asgard. With his two wolves at his feet, and his two ravens, Thought and Memory, on his shoulders, he surveyed all the nine worlds.

As the sun rose, Odin sent Thought and Memory out across the universe. The ravens visited the nine worlds, questioning the living and the dead. Then they returned at nightfall and whispered in Odin's ear all they had seen and heard.

But one day, Odin decided that he had to gain for himself all the world's wisdom and memory. To achieve this, he had to drink from the magic waters of Mimir's Well.

Odin set out from Asgard and traveled to Jotunheim, the land of the frost-giants. When he arrived at the magic well, Odin stood before the enormous head of the god Mimir. Though Mimir's head had been severed from his body in the war between the Aesir and the Vanir gods, he still had great wisdom and memory and the power of speech.

"I must have a drink from your well," said Odin.

"Indeed?" asked Mimir. "Even a god must sacrifice something in exchange for a drink from my waters."

"Tell me what you wish me to sacrifice," said Odin.

"You must give me one of your eyes," said Mimir.

"An eye is small price to pay for all the wisdom and memory of the nine worlds," said Odin.

Odin plucked out one eye and gave it to Mimir. In exchange, Mimir gave him a drink from his magic well.

II. THE QUEST FOR THE SECRET RUNES

Now Odin was pleased to have all the wisdom and memory of the nine worlds. Yet he wished to have more. He wanted to learn the secret runes — mysterious, written symbols that gave one magic powers over nature.

Odin knew that the price of great knowledge was great suffering, so he hung for nine days from the World Tree. With his own sword piercing his side, he swung in the windy dark, yearning for food and drink.

Tortured and alone, Odin gazed down into the world of the dead, and slowly he perceived eighteen runes. Thus, he learned how to calm storms, heal the sick, speak to the dead, and forecast the future.

Afterward, Odin carved the mysterious runes into wood and stone and bone. He carved them into the paw of the bear, the claws of the wolf, the beak of the eagle. He carved them into the end of the rainbow. In this way, he passed the runes on to men, so that they, too, could learn the secrets of nature.

III. THE QUEST FOR POETRY

Now Odin had all the wisdom and memory of the nine worlds. He was a master magician and lord of the runes. But still, he thirsted for one thing more — the Mead of Poetry, a special drink that turned one into a poet. Odin believed that being a good poet was as important as being a good warrior. For anyone who could use words in beautiful and imaginative ways would surely have mastery over all life.

Long before, the Mead of Poetry had been stolen from the dwarves by the giant Suttung. Hidden deep in a mountain cave, it was guarded day and night by Suttung's daughter.

One morning, with a patch over one eye and disguised in a black cape and a wide-brimmed hat, Odin set out for the land of the giants. Soon after he arrived in Jotunheim, he came upon nine trolls cutting wheat in a field.

Odin offered to sharpen the trolls' cutting tools. When they said yes, he pulled his whetstone from his belt and put a razor-sharp edge on all their blades.

The trolls were so impressed that they demanded the whetstone for themselves.

"Whoever can catch it, can have it!" said Odin, throwing the stone into the air.

The greedy trolls fell upon one another, fighting over the whetstone, until soon they were all slain by each other's sharp blades.

Odin continued on his journey, until he came to the home of Suttung's brother, Baugi.

"My name is Bolverk," Odin said. Bolverk means *one who can do the most difficult tasks.* "May I stay here and work for you?"

"Indeed. I do need help," said Baugi. "My nine troll workers had a quarrel this afternoon, and they all killed one another."

"Do not worry," said Odin. "I will do the work of all nine. But in exchange, you must give me the Mead of Poetry which your brother, Suttung, stole from the dwarves."

"Of course!" said Baugi. He thought the mead was a small payment, for like most giants, he did not particularly value the gift of poetry.

Odin cut wheat all summer, easily doing the work of the nine trolls. Baugi was very pleased, and once the wheat was harvested, he hurried to his brother to ask for the Mead of Poetry.

But Suttung did not want to part with the magic liquid because he knew it was important to the gods. The stubborn giant refused all his brother's entreaties and ordered him to leave.

Baugi was angry when he returned home.

"Don't worry, we will outwit your brother," said Odin. "Help me bore a hole into the mountain where the mead is hidden, and I will convince Suttung's daughter to give me the drink."

Baugi helped Odin bore a deep hole through the hard mountain rock. Then Odin turned himself into a snake and slithered through the hole into the hidden cavern.

Odin quickly turned himself back into a god, and he won over Suttung's daughter, Gunlod. He stayed with the maiden giant for three days, and each day, drank a barrel of mead.

On the fourth day, inspired by the fiery drink of poetry, Odin turned into an eagle. He spread his mighty wings and soared home to Asgard. Suttung soon learned of Odin's theft. He swiftly donned an eagle's disguise and set off for Asgard as well.

Suttung's pursuit was in vain, though. For when the gods saw the first eagle flying toward their home, they knew it was Odin.

Quickly they grabbed all the jars they could find and set them on the ground.

Odin opened his beak, and the magic liquid poured down from the sky into the jars of the gods.

From then on, the art of poetry was known as Odin's Gift, and the great god Odin shared it with all the gods and humans who had the wit and wisdom to make good use of it.

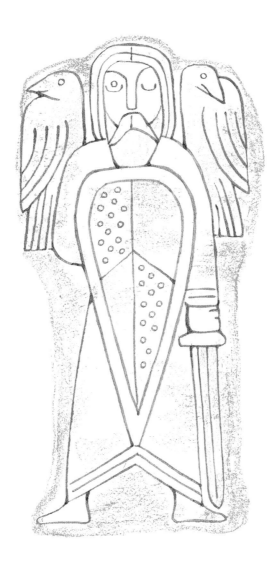

THREE

THE MAGIC STALLION

Of all the gods
Is Odin the greatest
And Sleipnir the best of the steeds.

THE GOD LOKI WAS THE MOST DANGEROUS of all the gods, not because he was brutal and strong, but because he was charming and sly and cunning. Again and again, Loki led the gods into trouble, then used his charm and sly magic to save them. Such became the case in the early days of the universe when a mysterious stranger appeared in Asgard.

The stranger offered to rebuild the wall that had been destroyed in the war between the Aesir and Vanir.

The gods and goddesses were eager to have their wall rebuilt, for they felt defenseless against any mountain-giants or frost-giants who might try to invade their land.

"I'll rebuild your fortress in exchange for three things," said the stranger, "the sun, the moon, and the goddess Freya."

The gods were startled by this request. They could not imagine losing their beloved Freya or the world's light. They quickly held a council. As soon as they came up with a plan, they called the stranger before them.

"If you rebuild our wall, we will give you the goddess Freya and the sun and the moon. But you must begin the first day of winter and finish by the first day of summer, or you will lose your reward."

The gods were certain no one could build a wall around Asgard in such a short period of time.

"May I have the use of my stallion?" said the stranger.

The gods were just about to say no when the mischief-maker, Loki, stepped forth. "Of course," Loki said to the stranger. "Why not?"

"If Thor were here, he'd never allow this stranger to have his way," grumbled one of the gods. The mighty Thor was in the eastern region at the time, fighting trolls.

"Don't worry about Thor," said Loki. "The help of this builder's stallion will make little difference."

After the sun set on the first night of winter, the stranger began working with the help of his stallion. By the following day, the gray horse had hauled many huge stones.

"Indeed that horse must be magic," said one of the gods.

"And his owner must be a giant," said another. "For only a giant would be so crafty."

Night after night, the gods watched in horror as the giant and his stallion worked on the Asgard wall. Just three days before summer was to begin, their work was nearly completed.

The gods met in their council.

"What will we do?" said one. "We're going to lose Freya and the sun and the moon!"

"How did this happen?" said another.

"Loki is responsible!" said still another. "His advice always gets us into trouble!"

"Put him to death! Losing the sun and moon is unbearable! Losing Freya even more so!"

The gods dragged Loki before them. "You must find a way to save us from the giant!" one god said.

"Or we'll turn you over to Thor when he comes home — and he'll kill you!" another god threatened.

Loki fell to his knees. "Please spare me!" he begged. "I promise I'll find a way to save Freya and the sun and moon!"

That night, as the giant and his stallion were gathering the last stones for the Asgard wall, a beautiful mare suddenly appeared in the moonlight. She whinnied to the giant's stallion.

The stallion broke free of his harness and bounded to the mare's side. Together the stallion and the mare galloped into the woods.

The giant shouted angrily and ran after his horse. He chased after him all night, but could not catch him.

The next night, the same thing happened. The stallion ran away with the mare, and no stones were hauled.

The next night, the same thing happened again.

When the giant realized his wall was not going to be finished in time, he flew into a rage. He stormed around Asgard, threatening to destroy everything.

At that moment, the mighty Thor was on his way home after defeating the trolls in the East. When Thor heard the giant shouting, he hurried to help the gods.

Thor gave one blow to the giant's head and shattered his skull into a thousand pieces. The giant died instantly — and Freya, the sun, and the moon were saved.

Some months later, Loki miraculously gave birth to a colt. The little horse was gray and looked exactly like the giant's stallion — except the colt had eight legs and could fly through the air and gallop over the sea.

The gods called the colt Sleipnir, which means "slipper," and Odin took him for his own steed.

From that time on, Sleipnir was the greatest horse in all the nine worlds.

HOW THOR GOT HIS HAMMER

Northward a hall
In Nidavellir
Of gold there rose
For Sindri's race.

THOR WAS THE STRONGEST OF ALL THE GODS. He had a red beard and fiery eyes and rode in a chariot drawn by two goats. Thor was very quick to lose his temper, but he was equally quick to get it back again.

Thor's wife, Sif, had the most beautiful hair in all the universe. Made of gold, Sif's hair gleamed like summer wheat blowing in the wind.

One night while Sif slept, the mischief-maker, Loki, crept into her chamber and cut off all her hair.

When Sif woke up and discovered her hair was gone, she screamed, then collapsed with grief.

Thor flew into a rage and searched everywhere for Loki, for he knew this was the work of the trickster. When he finally found Loki, Thor threatened to kill him.

"No, please! Spare me!" Loki cried. "I'll restore Sif's hair! I promise it will be more beautiful than before!"

"Do as you promise," growled Thor. "Or I will slay you with my own hands."

Loki scampered away from Thor and hurried to Nidavellir, the world of the dwarves. He went straight to the cave of some dwarves, who were known as Ivaldi's sons.

"You must make new hair for the goddess Sif," Loki commanded Ivaldi's sons.

Eager to win favor with the gods, the dwarves set to work at once and spun beautiful golden hair for Sif.

"We have two other gifts for the gods as well," said one dwarf. He then presented Loki with a ship made of gold and said, "Please give this boat to Frey. On the sea, it will bring forth a good breeze all by itself and will carry as many sailors as Frey wishes. On land, it can be folded up and carried in his pocket."

Another dwarf gave Loki a shining spear. "Take this magic spear to Odin," he said. "Nothing can keep it from hitting its target."

Loki thanked the dwarves, then set off for home.

But on his way back to Asgard, a sneaky idea came to Loki. And he quickly turned around and hurried back to Nidavellir.

Soon he came to the cave of two dwarves named Sindri and Brok. "Look at these amazing gifts!" Loki said to the two dwarves. "The sons of Ivaldi have made them for the gods. I'll bet you cannot do as well. In fact, I'll wager my own head that you can't."

"Your head?"

"Indeed, you may cut off my head, but you must not injure any other part of me."

"Okay, good. Let's get to work," Sindri said to Brok. "Not only will we prove we can do better work than Ivaldi's sons, but we'll have the pleasure of lopping off this mischief-maker's head."

Sindri placed a pig's skin in the furnace, then gave Brok a pair of bellows. "While I'm out of the room, pump the fire," he said. "If you stop, it will not be hot enough and all will be lost."

As Brok pumped the bellows, Loki feared that these dwarves might win the wager. So he quickly changed into a fly and bit Brok's hand.

Brok cried out in pain, but still he kept pumping the bellows.

When Sindri returned and lifted the pig's skin from the fire, Loki cried out with astonishment. The pig's skin had been changed into a golden boar with a gleaming mane and bristles.

Sindri then placed a lump of gold into the furnace and commanded Brok to fan the fire.

As Brok pumped the bellows, Loki changed into a fly again and bit Brok's neck.

Though Brok cried out in agony, he kept pumping the bellows.

When Sindri returned, he took the lump of gold from the fire. Loki gasped, for the lump had been changed into a glittering golden arm-ring.

Sindri next placed a piece of iron into the fire. "Pump again," he told Brok.

While Brok pumped the bellows, Loki changed into a fly for the third time and bit Brok on his eyelids.

Brok shouted with pain, but still, he kept working. And when Sindri took the iron from his fire, he held up an enormous silver hammer.

"Take these three gifts to Asgard," said Sindri. "And let the gods say who are the best craftsmen."

When Loki and Brok journeyed together to Asgard, the gods and goddesses gathered in their council.

"Now you must say which gifts are better," said Loki. "Those made by the sons of Ivaldi. Or those made by Sindri and Brok."

First Loki presented Sif with her new golden hair. "Place this hair on your head," he told her, "and it will magically start growing from your scalp."

Sif did as Loki said, and her new hair gleamed in the torchlight. Indeed, it was more beautiful than her own hair.

Next, Loki gave the magic spear to Odin and the magic boat to Frey, and the gods and goddesses greatly admired both gifts.

But then Brok stepped forward. "These gifts are from Sindri and myself," he said.

First the dwarf presented Frey with the golden boar. "This boar will run through air and over the water faster than any horse. Wherever he goes he will give light to the dark."

Next Brok presented the golden arm-ring to Odin. "This gold will keep making gold for you," he said. "Eight rings of the same weight will drop from this ring every ninth night."

Finally Brok presented the huge hammer to Thor. "You may strike this hammer as hard as you please and it will never be damaged. It never misses its target and it always returns to your hand."

Thor bowed before the dwarf. "Thank you for the most important gift of all," he said. "Now I can protect Asgard from the giants."

"Indeed," said Odin. "It is clear that Brok and Sindri have outdone the sons of Ivaldi."

The gods and goddesses cheered.

"And it is also clear that Loki has lost his wager," said Thor.

Before Loki could scamper away, Thor grabbed him by the hair. Then Brok held a knife to Loki's neck.

"I'm afraid Brok must take your head off now," Thor said to Loki.

"Ah, of course," said Loki. "But remember, Brok, I said you could only cut off my head as long as you did not injure any other part of me — and that includes my neck!"

When Brok realized that this feat was impossible, he was forced to let Loki go.

Indeed, the gods and goddesses were even a bit grateful to Loki. Though he'd brought them terrible grief, he'd made up for it by bringing them many amazing gifts, including the most wondrous gift of all — Thor's mighty hammer.

LOKI'S CHILDREN

The fetters shall break
And the wolf run free.
Secret things I know
And onward I see
The doom of the powers,
The gods of war.

ONE DAY, THE GODS RECEIVED WORD that Loki had fathered three children in Jotunheim, world of the frost-giants. Greatly alarmed, the gods gathered by the Well of Urd, also known as the Well of Fate. There, the gods met with three maidens called Norns.

The Norns could see what the future held for all the gods and humans. At every birth, they predicted whether the baby would have a pleasant life or a hard one, a long life or a short one.

Now the gods asked the Norns to predict the future of Loki's children.

"All three of these children will bring great harm to you someday," warned the first Norn.

"One of them will cause Odin's death in the last battle of the world," said the second Norn.

"Another will bring about Thor's death," said the third Norn.

Stunned by this news, Odin called his warriors together. He ordered them to go to the land of the giants and find Loki's children.

Soon Odin's army returned with three gruesome creatures. The first was a mighty wolf called Fenrir. The second was a terrible snake called the Midgard Serpent. The third was a monster named Hel.

Odin immediately tossed the serpent into the sea. When the snake landed in the water, he grew so long that his body encircled all of Midgard, the land of humans.

Odin next grabbed the monster Hel by the neck. She was pink from her head to her waist and blue-black from her waist to her feet. Odin threw Hel into Niflheim, the frozen region of the dead. In Niflheim, Hel became ruler of the dead. She set up a home for all mortals who had died of sickness or old age. Her palace was called Sleet-Cold; her table was called Hunger; and her bed, Disease.

Odin next turned his attention to the wolf, Fenrir. "This one I believe is the most dangerous of all," said Odin. "For this reason he will remain in Asgard, so we can all keep an eye on him."

Taking care of Fenrir was very difficult, for each day the beast grew stronger and more fierce.

When the gods met again beside the Well of Urd, the Norns gave them a severe warning: "This is the very one who is fated to cause your final destruction!" the first Norn said to Odin.

"You must control him forever," said the second Norn.

"Find a way to bind his power once and for all," said the third.

Odin ordered his men to make the strongest iron chain possible to bind Fenrir.

But no sooner had they chained the wolf than he broke free.

The gods made a second iron chain, twice as strong as the first.

But the wolf's strength doubled, and as soon as he was chained, he broke free once again.

Finally, the gods bound Fenrir with a third chain. This chain was three times as strong as the first.

Again, the wolf's strength tripled, and he broke free once more.

The gods feared they would never be able to bind Fenrir, so they called for Frey's messenger, Skirnir.

"Go to the world of the dark elves and find a magic fetter to bind this wolf," Odin told Skirnir.

Skirnir left Asgard and journeyed to Svartalfheim, the world of the dark elves. He hurried to an underground cave of the elves and demanded a fetter that could not be broken.

The dark elves disappeared into the back of their cave. Moments later they returned with a silken ribbon.

"This fetter is made of six impossible things," one said. "The noise of a cat's foot-fall, the beard of a woman, the roots of a rock, the sinews of a bear, the breath of a fish, and the spittle of a bird."

Skirnir carried the magic fetter back to Asgard. The gods thanked him profusely. Then they journeyed in a boat to the rocky island where the mighty wolf lived.

"Let us bind you with this silken fetter," Odin said to Fenrir. "If you cannot break it, we'll have no reason to fear you, and we'll set you free."

"How can I be certain that you'll set me free?" said the wolf. "One of you must lay your hand in my mouth to prove your good faith."

Tyr, one of the bravest gods, stretched out his right hand and laid it in the wolf's mouth. Then the gods wrapped the magic fetter around the wolf's body and bound his feet.

When the wolf lashed out, the ribbon did not break. The more Fenrir struggled, the tighter the fetter became. When all the gods laughed, the enraged wolf bit off Tyr's hand.

But Fenrir was conquered. The gods tied the fetter to a chain and fixed the chain to a great rock. Frothing at the mouth, the wolf created a mighty foaming river. He howled and foamed until the end of the nine worlds.

The god Tyr was honored forevermore for sacrificing his right hand for the good of all.

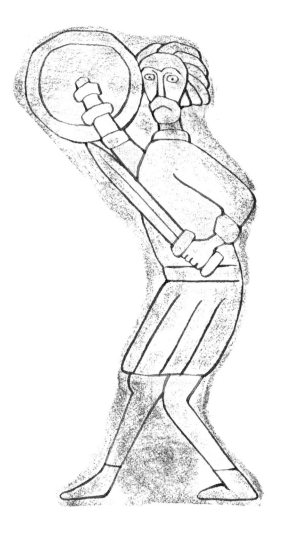

THE GIANT'S BRIDE

Spake then Thrym,
The lord of giants:
"Whoever saw a damsel
Eat so bravely?
Never have I seen one
Bite so boldly,
Nor a maiden quaff
More cups of mead!"

MIGHTY THOR CARRIED HIS MAGIC HAMMER everywhere he went. Whenever he swung it, lightning bolts streaked across the sky. When he struck it against the rocks, thunder rumbled, shaking the earth. For this reason, Thor was called the Thunder God.

But one day Thor woke up and discovered that his precious hammer was missing. Believing Loki might be up to his mischief again, he quickly called for the trickster.

Loki assured Thor that he was innocent, and to prove it, he said he would travel to the world of the frost-giants.

Loki borrowed Freya's falcon disguise. Then he lifted into the air and flew far over the nine worlds to the land of the giants.

There, Loki found Thrym, the king of the giants, sitting on top of a hill, stroking his horse.

"What's the matter?" Thrym said. "Why have you come alone to our land?"

"Because I believe you have Thor's hammer," said Loki.

"Yes, I have it," said Thrym. "I've hidden it eight miles under the earth. I'll only give it back if you give me Freya for my wife."

Loki flew back to the realm of the gods and delivered this news to Thor. Then the two hurried to Freya.

"Put on your bridal veil!" Loki ordered the beautiful goddess. "You must marry the giant Thrym or the gods will come to a terrible end!"

"Never!" cried Freya. "I will never marry that hideous giant!"

The gods and goddesses were quickly called together in a council.

"How can we get my hammer back?" asked Thor.

"*You* yourself must go to the giants wearing bridal clothes," Heimdall answered.

"Me?" roared Thor. "You want *me* to dress up as a bride?"

"Silence, Thor," said Odin. "You must do as Heimdall says, or the giants will conquer Asgard with your hammer."

Thor's face grew red as the gods dressed him in a wedding dress. They placed a pretty cap on his head and put Freya's necklace around his neck. Then they hung a woman's house keys from his waist.

"I will go with you as your maidservant," said Loki. And he also disguised himself in woman's clothing.

Thor hitched his two goats to his chariot. Then he and Loki soared over the mountains to the land of the giants.

"Hearken, giants!" cried Thrym to his kin. "Put straw on the benches! I see my bride is arriving!"

The king of the giants gloated as he escorted Thor from the goat-driven chariot. "Gold-horned cattle I have," said Thrym. "Jet-black oxen and many gems and jewels I have. You, my dear, were the only treasure I did not have — until now."

As the sun set over the kingdom of Thrym, the giants guzzled kegs of ale and ate a whole ox. All the while, Thrym could not keep his eyes off his new bride.

"Whoever saw a bride eat more?" he said to his men. "Or a maiden drink more?"

"My mistress has not eaten in eight days," Loki said in a high voice. "She was too excited about her impending marriage."

Longing to kiss Freya, Thrym peeked beneath her veil.

But when the giant saw his new bride's eyes, he screamed and leapt back the entire length of his hall. "Her eyes!" he said, trembling. "Her eyes burn like fire!"

Again Loki spoke in his high voice: "Her eyes burn because she has not slept for eight nights, and because her desire for you is so great."

Thrym relaxed a bit. "Very well then," he said, "bring forth Thor's hammer. Give it to me so I can bless my bride."

The giants brought Thor's mighty hammer into the hall, and the god's heart leapt with joy when he saw his magic weapon again.

"Let it rest on my bride's knees while we promise our marriage vows to one another," said Thrym.

As soon as the giants placed the hammer on Thor's knees, Thor grabbed it. He bellowed with rage; then he stood up and began swinging. The Thunder God killed Thrym first, then one giant after the next.

After Thor had slain many giants, he and Loki jumped into the goat chariot and carried Thor's precious hammer back to the land of the gods.

THE GOLDEN APPLES

Thrymheim 'tis called
Where Thiazi dwelt
He the hideous giant.

ONE DAY, ODIN AND LOKI WERE RETURNING to Asgard from a trip over the mountains. Since they were having trouble finding food, they were thrilled when they finally came upon a herd of oxen in the valley. Immediately they killed an ox and prepared a fire to cook it.

But a strange thing happened. As the gods roasted the ox over the fire, they discovered that no matter how long they cooked it, it remained raw.

"What does this mean?" said Odin.

"It means I have prevented your fire from cooking the ox," said a deep voice.

The voice seemed to be coming from an enormous eagle sitting in a nearby tree. Actually, the eagle was the giant Thiazi in disguise.

"If you let me eat my fill," said the eagle, "I will make the fire cook your ox."

The gods were so hungry that they quickly agreed. And the eagle coasted down to the ground, then made the fire burn the ox. When the ox was cooked, Thiazi began to eat. He ate and ate and ate.

Angered by such greediness, Loki snatched a long, sharp stick and stabbed the eagle. Loki's weapon stuck into the bird's back, and as the eagle flew up from the ground, he carried Loki away.

The eagle dragged Loki over rock heaps and trees. Afraid his arms might be ripped from his body, Loki begged for help.

"I'll free you only under one condition," said the eagle.

"Anything!" cried Loki.

"You must lure Idun out of Asgard with her basket of apples."

"I can't do that!" said Loki. The goddess Idun guarded the golden apples of youth. Whenever the gods and goddesses started to grow old, they took a bite of Idun's apples and were instantly made young again.

"Do as I say — or you will die!" said Thiazi.

Loki did not want to die, so he agreed to help Thiazi if Thiazi would first release him.

The eagle released him, and Loki tumbled to earth.

Soon after the gods returned home, Loki went to Idun. "I've found some wonderful apples in the forest," he said.

"Indeed?" said she.

"Yes, bring your apples and we'll compare them. If those apples are better than yours, we'll pick them and carry them home."

Idun agreed to do as the trickster said, and she carried her basket of apples into the forest.

Idun and Loki had not traveled far when Thiazi suddenly swooped down in his eagle disguise. The giant snatched Idun and her apples.

Then he carried them back to Thrymheim, his hall in the land of the giants.

The gods were horrified when Idun failed to return home that night. Since her golden apples of youth were no longer in Asgard, the gods all began to wither and wrinkle with age.

In a panic, they met in their council.

"When did you last see Idun?" each asked the other.

"I saw her walking into the woods with Loki," said one.

"Seize the scoundrel!" said Odin.

When Loki was brought before the council, he shook with fear.

"You will be put to a slow tortuous death, Loki, if you do not tell us what happened to Idun," said Odin.

"She's imprisoned in Thrymheim," said Loki, trembling, "but I promise I'll save her."

"You must save her at once, or we'll all die soon of old age!" cried a god.

"Lend me your falcon suit, Freya," said Loki, "so I can fly to Jotunheim as quickly as possible."

The goddess Freya handed over her feather suit, and Loki put it on and flew to the land of the giants.

When Loki arrived at Thrymheim, the home of Thiazi, he found Idun there alone. Thiazi was out at sea.

As soon as Loki saw Idun, he cast a spell over her and changed her into a nut. He then clutched the nut with his talons and started back to Asgard.

When Thiazi returned home and found Idun missing, he became enraged. He donned his own plumage and flew after Loki. Thiazi's wings made a terrible rushing sound as he soared through the air to Asgard.

When the gods and goddesses heard the sound of Thiazi's wings, they looked up at the sky and saw an eagle chasing a falcon. They knew at once the eagle was Thiazi and the falcon, Loki; and they quickly built a woodpile.

As soon as Loki passed beyond the walls of Asgard, the gods set fire to their wood.

Flames roared skyward, but Thiazi was flying so swiftly he couldn't stop himself in time, and he sailed directly into the fire.

His bright feathers in flames, Thiazi fell to the ground. When he landed within the walls of Asgard, Odin killed him.

Loki pulled off his falcon costume. He said a spell over the enchanted nut, and it instantly changed back into Idun.

The guardian of the magic apples was saved — and so was the eternal youth of the gods and goddesses.

EIGHT

THE FAIREST FEET

Thiazi I slew,
Strong-souled giant,
And flung his eyes up
Where men shall behold them
In the shining heavens above.

SKADI, THE DAUGHTER of the slain giant Thiazi, waited day after day for her father's return. When news of his death finally reached her, she flew into a rage. She grabbed a sword and shield and strode to Asgard to avenge Thiazi's death.

Heimdall, the guard at the entrance to Asgard, saw the giantess coming, and he called out a warning to the gods.

Odin and his warriors hurried to the gate. "Put your weapon away!" Odin bellowed to Skadi. "Enough blood has been spilled!"

"No, I have come for revenge!" she shouted, waving her sword.

"I'm sorry I had to slay your father!" said Odin. "Let me show my regrets by offering you a gift instead of a battle. What do you want?"

Skadi put down her sword and stared long and hard at Odin. "Give me a husband," she said coldly.

Odin breathed a sigh of relief. "That is not a difficult request. Of course we can give you a husband," he said.

"But I must choose him for myself!" said Skadi.

The gods mumbled fearfully among themselves. "What if she chooses Balder for her husband?" they asked Odin.

Odin was loathe to give his most-adored son to the giantess. He thought for a long moment, then turned back to Skadi. "All right. You may choose your husband from among all of us," he told her. "But you can only choose him by the look of his feet."

Skadi agreed to Odin's proposal, for she was certain she would be able to recognize the feet of the most beautiful god. All the gods stood behind a curtain, completely covered except for their feet. Skadi walked up and down before them, searching for Balder.

Suddenly the giantess let out a cry and pointed to the fairest feet of all. They were perfectly sculpted and as smooth and lovely as marble.

These feet must belong to Balder, thought Skadi.

But when the god uncovered his face, she saw it was not Balder at all, but Njord, the ruler of the sea. Over time, Njord's feet had been worn smooth by the wind and waves.

At first Skadi was disappointed, but when she looked into the warm blue eyes of the god, her icy heart gave way.

"I will take Njord for my husband," the giantess said to Odin. "But before I can be his wife, you must give me something else."

"What?" said Odin.

"You must give me back my laughter. Since my father's death, I have not been able to laugh."

Odin felt Skadi's deep sorrow as keenly as if it were his own, and he agreed to restore her laughter.

Loki suddenly came forward. He pulled out a rope and tied one end to a goat and the other to himself, and the two began playing tug-of-war.

As all the gods and goddesses laughed, Skadi joined in. Despite her terrible grief, she could laugh again. And despite all the trouble Loki had caused, he was now forgiven.

When Skadi stopped laughing, she looked wistfully at Odin. "I still miss my father," she said.

"I know," said Odin. "And that's why I shall now give you *this* gift." He pulled two shining orbs from the folds of his robe. "Thiazi's eyes," he said. Then he hurled the eyes of the giant into the sky, and they became two glittering stars. "Now your father can look down on you whenever he wishes," said Odin.

After they wed, neither Skadi nor Njord wished to leave their own region. But finally they made a pact to live nine nights in Skadi's frozen mountains and three nights near Njord's warm sea.

To some in the northland, this explained why wintry storms raged for nine months of the year, and balmy, gentle weather prevailed for only three.

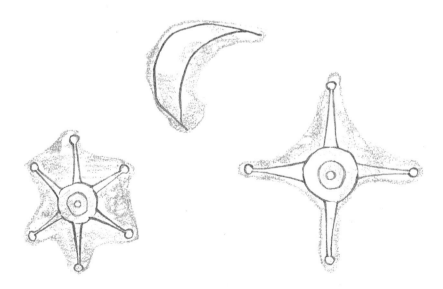

NINE

SPELL OF
THE GIANT KING

That thou hast fared
On the East-road forth
To men should'st thou say no more;
In the thumb of a glove
Didst thou hide, thou great one,
And there forgot thou was Thor.

ONE MORNING THOR WOKE UP feeling very feisty, and he decided
to travel to Utgard to fight some giants. Utgard was a fortress inside
Jotunheim, the land of giants. He asked Loki and two young servants
named Thialfi and Roskva to go with him. Then the four travelers
set off on a journey to Utgard.

By dark, Thor and his companions found themselves deep in a forest.
As they sought shelter for the night, they came upon a mysterious
house with five tunnel-like chambers.

Weary from their journey, they entered a side chamber of the house
and fell asleep immediately.

At midnight the group was awakened by a terrible rumbling. The
house was shaking as if in an earthquake.

When the sun rose, Thor and the others stepped outside and discovered the source of the rumbling and shaking: A giant was asleep and snoring on the ground.

"Wake up! Tell us your name!" Thor yelled at the giant.

The giant calmly opened his eyes and stared at Thor. "My name is Skrymir," he said. "And I see that your little group has trifled with my glove."

The giant picked up the strange dwelling that had sheltered Thor and the others, and he put it on his hand. Each chamber fit over one of his fingers, and the side chamber covered his thumb.

With a shock, Thor realized he'd spent the night in the thumb of a giant's glove!

"Now tell me, where are you going?" Skrymir asked Thor.

"Utgard," said Thor.

"What a coincidence. Me, too," said the giant. "May I travel with you?"

"I suppose," said Thor reluctantly.

"Good! I'll carry your provisions!" the giant said.

Before Thor could protest, the giant grabbed Thor's bag of food and put it inside his own bag. Then he began taking great strides, leading the group through the woods.

At sunset, Skrymir brought everyone to a shelter under a towering oak tree. Without bothering to eat, the giant crashed to the ground and began to snore loudly.

Thor and his companions were quite hungry, so Thor tried to pry open the giant's bag.

The bag, however, could not be opened. Thor kept trying until finally he lost his temper. He grabbed his hammer, stomped over to the giant, and hit him on the head.

Skrymir opened his eyes. "What happened?" he asked in a sleepy voice. "Did a little leaf fall on my head?"

Thor stepped away in confusion and waited for the giant to fall asleep again.

When the giant began snoring again, Thor rushed at him and hit him again with his hammer.

The giant opened his eyes again. "What happened?" he said. "Did a little acorn fall on my head?"

Thor's hammer had never failed to kill a giant before. He couldn't understand what was happening. He waited for the giant to fall asleep again. Then he rushed forward and used all his might to strike his hammer against the giant's head.

This time Skrymir sat up and stroked his cheek. "There must be birds in the tree above," he said. "I think they shook some dirt from a twig and it fell on me."

The giant stood up, threw the food bag over his shoulder, and strode away, leaving the others gaping in astonishment.

Thor stared at his hammer. Had his weapon lost all its magic?

Baffled by his defeat, Thor slowly led his companions deeper into the woods, until soon they came to the fortress of Utgard.

Thor stepped into a huge hall filled with giants.

"Who are you?" the king of the giants roared. "And what talents have you? We only allow the most clever and cunning to visit us."

Taken aback, Thor looked at his companions. "Well, Loki can eat faster than anyone in the nine worlds," he said.

"Ah, indeed?" The giant king ordered a giant named Logi to have an eating contest with Loki.

Loki and Logi sat at opposite ends of a long table, and the king's servants brought in enormous plates of meat.

The contest began! Loki gobbled the meat off the bones as fast as he could. When he finished, he saw that Logi had devoured all the bones — and the plates, too!

Thor was dismayed that Loki had lost the eating contest. "Well, my servant boy, Thialfi, can run faster than anyone in the nine worlds," he said.

"Indeed?" The giant king called for a boy giant named Hugi. "These two will race one another," he said.

Everyone went outside, and when the race began, Thialfi sprinted across a field as fast as he could. But Hugi ran much faster, so fast that he reached the end of the field before Thialfi was even halfway across.

Thor was very agitated. "Well, let me prove my talent for drinking!" he said.

A serving boy brought Thor a drinking horn. The god tilted his head back, and he drank and drank and drank.

But no matter how much mead Thor swallowed, the horn stayed full!

Finally Thor gave up and collapsed in exhaustion.

"It seems that none of you are as talented as you think," said the giant king. "However, I'll give you two more chances to show your powers."

The king brought out a gray cat. "Try to lift my cat from the floor," he challenged Thor.

Thor reached for the cat. But the cat arched his back so high that it formed a rainbow over Thor's head, and Thor could only lift one cat paw off the floor.

"Thor, you are a weakling compared to the giants!" roared the giant king.

Hearing these words, Thor's eyes flashed with anger, but the giant king didn't care.

"Your anger cannot harm us," said the king. "Perhaps I can find an old woman who will fight with you."

The king called for a feeble, old woman. She grabbed Thor and wrestled him to his knees; then she pinned him to the floor.

When Thor was completely humiliated by his defeat, the king leaned close to him. "Tell me, God of Thunder," he whispered, "has this trip turned out as you had imagined?"

Dumbstruck, Thor shook his head.

"Now I'll confess the truth, Thor," said the giant king. "Your strength is so great, I had to work magic spells to trick you. I was Skrymir, the giant in the forest. Each time you hit me, I caused your hammer to hit the ground instead. I put magic spells on my men to help them defeat Loki and Thialfi. And the drinking horn was dipped into the sea. You would be surprised to see how much seawater you actually drank."

"And the cat?" said Thor.

"Ah, the cat is a great wonder," said the king. "It wasn't a cat at all — but the Midgard Serpent that encircles the world! No one could believe that you actually lifted one paw off the ground."

"And the old woman?" said Thor.

"The old woman is Old Age itself," whispered the giant. "No one can defeat Old Age, Thor. And *you* will never defeat *me,* for I can always work my magic on you."

Thor exploded with fury. This was the first time in his life he'd been defeated by a giant. He grabbed his hammer and swung it at the giant king.

But the giant king vanished.

Thor whirled about, swinging his hammer, trying to hack down the castle of Utgard.

But in an instant, the castle vanished also. And Thor was left standing alone, swinging his hammer over an empty plain.

TEN

MARRIAGE OF THE ICE MAIDEN

Tell me, herdsman,
Who sitt'st on a hill
And watchest every way!
How, for Gymir's hounds,
Shall I win a word
With that giant's youthful maid?

NO ONE WAS ALLOWED TO SIT in Odin's high throne except Odin himself. But one day the god Frey entered Odin's hall, and when he saw that no one was about, he slipped into the god's high seat. From Odin's throne, Frey could see all the nine worlds.

As Frey surveyed Jotunheim, the cold, barren world of the frost-giants, his gaze rested on a great hall in the rocky hollow of an ice field. The hall belonged to Gymir, a fierce mountain giant.

Just then the doors to Gymir's hall swung open, and the giant's daughter, Gerd, stepped forth.

Gerd wore a white wool robe, and as she raised her arms to close the doors of the hall, she shone with such brilliance that the frigid world around her was bathed in a warm bronze light.

Frey felt as if he'd been struck like a bell. Trembling with desire, he slipped from Odin's high seat and returned to his own chambers.

Frey was so filled with longing for Gerd that he could not eat or sleep, or even speak. He knew the giantess was as cold and icy as she was beautiful, and she would never allow him to wed her.

Frey was the god of fertility. He sent sun and rain to the nine worlds. But now he refused to send any sunlight at all. He also refused to sprinkle the trees with rain or look after the harvests.

Frey's father, Njord, and all the gods grew worried. So Njord sent for Frey's courageous messenger, Skirnir.

"Please make my son talk to you, Skirnir," said Njord. "Find out what ails him. The worlds cannot survive without his help."

Skirnir hurried to Frey's chamber, where the god was grieving. "My prince," he said, kneeling before Frey. "Why are you lying here day after day? Tell me what is in your heart."

"My sorrow is so great I cannot even talk about it," said Frey.

"Try to remember the days when we were young and you told me everything," said Skirnir. "Please trust me now."

Frey sat up and looked at his old friend. "From Odin's high seat I saw the giantess Gerd. She is the most beautiful maiden in the nine worlds. Her gleaming light lit the sky and the sea. Now I can think of nothing but my longing for her."

Skirnir stood up and stroked his white beard. "This enthrallment must be your punishment for sitting on Odin's throne," he said.

"Perhaps," said Frey, "but it's too late to undo the harm now. If I cannot have Gerd for my wife, my heart will stay as frozen as the winter ground."

Skirnir sighed. "I will win this maiden for you," he said, "if you lend me the horse that leaps over the flames between our world and the world of the giants — and lend me the sword that fights by itself when a wise hand wields it."

Frey lent the two treasures to Skirnir, and the messenger hurried away.

Skirnir rode through the black sky, until he came to a wall of fire surrounding Gymir's realm. His mighty horse leapt through the flames with ease, then carried Skirnir to Gymir's bleak castle.

Surrounded by a high wall, the giant's home was guarded by a pair of fierce hounds chained to posts.

When Skirnir rode up on his horse, the dogs went mad, snarling and growling.

The messenger dismounted and stood in the cold wind and looked about. Spying a lone herdsman tending goats, he called out, "Tell me, sir, how can I get past these dogs and gain entry into the hall of Gymir?"

"Why do you need to enter that place?" asked the herdsman in a frightened voice.

"I must speak with the maiden Gerd."

"You have gone mad, my friend!" said the herdsman. "Ride away quickly! Before you end up in a grave! No one speaks to the ice maiden and lives!"

"My good man, it is better to be unafraid than to have a faint heart," said Skirnir. "The length of my life and the day of my death were decreed long ago." And with that, he strode over to the snarling hounds and spoke gently, trying to calm them.

Inside the great hall, Gerd called to her handmaiden, "Why do my dogs bark so?"

"A rider has come. Now he lets his horse graze on your land while he strokes your dogs," said the maid.

"Bid him come inside," said Gerd. "Give him ale to drink."

Skirnir entered the hall of Gymir. As he sipped his mead, Gerd appeared before him. "Who are you — an elf or god?" she asked. "And how did you come through the fire to our hall?"

"I'm not an elf, nor a child of two gods," said Skirnir. "I came magically through the fire to win your hand for the god Frey. He sends you these gifts — "

Before Gerd could speak, Skirnir brought out eleven golden apples.

"No one can buy me with apples," said Gerd. "Never will I live with the god Frey under one roof."

"Wait, he also sends you this magic ring that belongs to the gods. With this, you can make gold," he said.

"I don't want to make gold," said Gerd. "In my father's home, I have all the gold I want."

"Then take heed of *this* gift," said Skirnir, and he drew his sword. "With this, I'll cut off your head if you don't do as I say."

Gerd smiled. "I don't fear your sword," she said. "Remember, if you slay me, my father will kill you."

"Then listen carefully, dear Gerd," said Skirnir, and he reached into his cloak and pulled out a wand. "In the wet forest, I found this magic wand. If I strike you with it, you will be under a spell. You will find yourself on top of the eagle's hill, gazing at the land of the dead. The skin on your bones will become monstrous flesh. The gods will turn away from you, and you will spend all the rest of your days among hideous three-headed giants."

Gerd stared with horror at Skirnir, and her eyes filled with icy tears. "All right," she said in a brittle voice, "tell your master I will marry him in nine days, in the green forest of Barri."

Skirnir bowed slowly. Then he turned and strode out of the hall of Gymir.

Gerd's hounds were silent as the tall, white-bearded stranger mounted his black horse and galloped away across the forsaken landscape.

When Skirnir returned to Asgard, Frey rushed to greet him.

"She is yours," Skirnir said as he unbridled his panting horse.

"But how did you win her?" asked Frey.

Skirnir looked calmly at his master. "I am very persuasive," he told him.

Gerd was filled with cold fury when she went to the forest of Barri nine days later. The giant ice maiden could not believe she was being forced to marry the god of sunshine and rain.

But as soon as Gerd laid eyes on gentle, handsome Frey, her heart melted like the frozen ground beneath the summer sun. And as soon as she embraced him, flowers blossomed in all the fields.

ELEVEN

THE GIANT'S CAULDRON

Swelling with might
To the meeting of gods
Came Thor with the cauldron
Which Hymir had owned.
And the Holy Ones ever
Shall well drink ale
Each harvest of flax
In the Sea-God's hall.

ONE DAY AEGIR, THE LORD OF THE SEAS, invited the gods and goddesses to a great feast to celebrate the flax harvest. Soon after they arrived, Aegir discovered that he did not have a cauldron big enough to brew the gods' favorite ale.

Taking Thor aside, Aegir whispered, "Do you know where I can get a bigger cauldron?"

"Perhaps Tyr can help us," said Thor. "His father is a mountain giant who surely has a large cauldron."

"Oh, yes," said the god Tyr. "My father, Hymir, has a cauldron a mile deep. Unfortunately, he lives far away, near the borders of heaven."

"If we journey there together, do you think he will give it to us?" asked Thor.

"Oh, no," said Tyr. "He will not *give* it to us. He's very nasty and won't be at all happy to see us. Somehow we'll have to trick him."

Thor enjoyed tricking giants. So he and Tyr climbed into his goat-chariot and set out on the long journey to Hymir's hall.

Near the borders of heaven, they saw Tyr's grandmother — an ugly giantess with nine hundred heads. But as soon as they entered Hymir's hall, they were greeted kindly by Tyr's beautiful mother.

"My husband will be home soon from fishing," she said. "But sometimes he's cruel to unexpected guests. So you had better hide behind the wooden pillars at the end of the hall."

Thor and Tyr hid behind the pillars and waited for Hymir's return.

When the mountain giant soon entered the hall, his wife greeted him warmly. "Our son has come home!" she said. "He and a friend are waiting for you!"

As Hymir looked around for the visitors, his gaze was so cruel that the wooden pillars dissolved into splinters.

But the gods stepped forward bravely to greet him.

Hymir only glared at his son, Tyr, and the god Thor. Then he turned to a servant and ordered that three steers be roasted.

At dinner, Thor had such a great appetite that he ate two steers all by himself.

Hymir was not impressed. "You are very small and weak compared to the mountain giants," he said to Thor.

"Ah, then let me prove my strength," said Thor. "I will help you fish."

"Hah! You're too delicate to be of use to me," said Hymir. "You'll catch your death of cold if you travel with me to the region where I always fish."

Thor held his temper in check, though he was tempted to crash his

hammer against the rude giant's skull. "Oh, allow me to go fishing with you. Please, just once," he said.

Hymir finally relented, and the next morning, he and Thor set out together in his boat.

Thor rowed swiftly and far out to sea — farther, in fact, than Hymir himself had ever dared to go.

"Halt! Or we'll meet with terrible danger!" said the giant. He knew that the Midgard Serpent, the most hideous monster of the nine worlds, lived in this far region of the sea. But Thor rowed a bit farther before he anchored the boat and began to fish.

Hymir soon caught two whales. As the mountain giant pulled up his catch, Thor baited his line with a bull's head. The bait sank down to the bottom of the sea, and the Midgard Serpent grabbed it.

Thor used all his power to hold onto his catch. He pulled and pulled, until finally he pulled the terrible monster up from the deep.

As Thor struck the serpent with his hammer, the wind howled and the earth trembled. He was about to strike the monster one last time, but the frightened giant, Hymir, quickly drew his knife and cut Thor's fishing line.

The Midgard Serpent slipped away. As it sank to the bottom of the sea, Thor bellowed with anger and struck the giant on the ear. Little did Thor know that one day he would fight the Midgard Serpent again — this time, to the death.

Hymir the giant sullenly rubbed his sore ear as Thor rowed the fishing boat back across the sea.

Thor and Hymir returned to the giant's hall and joined Tyr and his mother for dinner. While they ate, Hymir admitted that Thor had shown great strength at sea.

"But there is one thing I know you cannot do," the giant said. "I know you cannot break my goblet."

Hymir handed Thor his heavy drinking cup and Thor threw it

against one of the pillars in the hall. Though the cup went straight through the wood, it did not even show the slightest crack.

Hymir's wife leaned close to Thor. "Hurl it at his head," she whispered. "His head is harder than a stone. Surely the cup will break."

Thor picked up the goblet again and hurled it against the giant's forehead. Though the goblet broke into a thousand pieces, the giant's head was unharmed.

"Well done," said Hymir. "But there is one thing I'm certain you cannot do."

"What is that?" asked Thor.

"You cannot lift my cauldron," said Hymir.

The giant led Thor and Tyr to his mile-deep cauldron, the biggest cauldron in the world.

Tyr tried to lift the cauldron first. The god huffed and puffed, but he was not able to even budge his father's cauldron.

Thor took over. He moaned and groaned. He exerted so much pressure that his feet crashed through the floor. Suddenly he lifted the cauldron into the air. Holding the mile-deep cauldron over his head, he started out of Hymir's hall.

The giant was speechless.

But as Thor and Tyr strode toward the goat-chariot, they heard angry shouting. They looked around and saw Hymir leading a mob of mountain-giants against them.

Thor put down his mighty cauldron. He took up his hammer and began swinging it. He killed one giant, then another and another — until Hymir and the few giants who were left ran for their lives.

Thor and Tyr then climbed into Thor's chariot. But the two goats, strong as they were, could not pull the mile-deep cauldron behind them. So Thor had to lift it above his head and carry it all the way home.

Not until he arrived in the realm of Aegir did Thor finally put down his cauldron. From then on, at every harvest, the lord of the sea had plenty of ale for all the gods and goddesses.

TWELVE

THOR AND THE CLAY GIANT

Dost tell how we once fought,
I and Hrungnir,
That hard-hearted giant
With a head made of stone?
Yet did he fall
And bow before me.

ONCE, WHILE THOR WAS AWAY KILLING TROLLS, Odin rode his horse Sleipnir to the land of the giants. As Odin wandered the desolate countryside, he came upon Hrungnir, the strongest of all the giants, whose head and heart were made of stone.

"What sort of horse is that?" asked Hrungnir, pointing at Odin's eight-legged steed.

"His name is Sleipnir," said Odin. "I wager there's not a faster horse in the nine worlds."

"I accept your wager," said Hrungnir, "for *I* have Goldfax, the fastest horse in the nine worlds."

Hrungnir jumped on Goldfax and galloped away. Odin spurred

Sleipnir and raced ahead of the giant. Whenever Hrungnir reached the top of a hill, he saw Sleipnir flying ahead of them.

The two horses flew like the wind, until Goldfax galloped after Sleipnir through the gates of Asgard.

The gods were surprised to see the giant Hrungnir enter their land. But they greeted him warmly and offered him mead.

Hrungnir drank the mead until he had drunk too much. Then he became rude and boastful. "I could take over your kingdom if I wanted to!" he said. "I could kill all of you! I could steal Freya and Sif and marry them!" He laughed loudly.

The gods were angry. But they didn't know how to get rid of the giant because he was too big and dangerous.

Finally a messenger was sent to find Thor and bring him home. The gods knew Thor was the only one among them who was strong enough to fight the arrogant giant.

When Thor returned to Asgard, he heard Hrungnir shouting and bragging. Thor raised his hammer to slay the giant.

But Hrungnir shot Thor a look filled with malice. "You will be a coward, Thor, if you try to kill me now, for I have no weapons. Let me return home and get my shield and whetstone. Then meet me in the valley of Jotunheim, and we'll see who's the stronger."

After Hrungnir hastened back to Jotunheim, all the frost-giants met to discuss the impending duel. They knew that if Thor was defeated, the giants could take over the land of the gods. But if Hrungnir lost the battle, Thor might try to take on the rest of the giants as well.

The giants came up with a plan to help Hrungnir win: They would make a giant out of clay. Then, when Thor hurled his hammer at the false giant, Hrungnir would step out from behind it and strike Thor with his whetstone.

The giants quickly made a clay figure nine miles high and three miles wide.

But Thor was not fooled. As soon as he and his servant, Thialfi, entered the valley of Jotunheim, he guessed the giants' trick.

"I can see Hrungnir hiding behind a clay figure," he said to Thialfi. "Let's do this. . . ." And he whispered a plan in Thialfi's ear.

Soon the giants heard Thor's servant yelling, and they saw him running across the valley.

"Why is your shield in front of you, Hrungnir?" cried Thialfi. "Thor has seen you! And now he is coming to meet you from below the earth!"

"Really?" said Hrungnir. And he quickly threw his shield down to the ground and stood on it to protect himself from Thor.

But the Thunder God did not rise from the ground. Instead, bolts of lightning flashed through the sky, and the earth trembled as Thor came striding furiously toward Hrungnir.

Thor hurled his mighty hammer at Hrungnir, and the giant flung his whetstone. When the giant's weapon struck the hammer in midair, the whetstone burst into two parts. One fell to earth and became a mountain. The other pierced Thor's head, and he fell to the ground.

At the same moment, Thor's hammer crashed into Hrungnir's head. It cracked his skull and killed him. As the giant crashed to earth, his foot landed on Thor's neck.

Thialfi tried to lift the huge foot off Thor's neck, but the servant boy was not strong enough.

All the gods tried to lift the giant's foot. But none were strong enough.

"Let me try," said Thor's son, Magni.

Magni was only three days old, but he was an enormous baby. Slowly, he lifted the giant's foot off his father's neck. And Thor stumbled up from the ground.

Thor embraced Magni and praised him highly. He rewarded Magni by giving him Goldfax, Hrungnir's horse.

Thor was in great pain after he returned home, for the piece of whetstone was still lodged in his head.

He sent for a wise woman named Groa, who sang magic spells over him and finally loosened the stone.

But then Thor did a foolish thing: He was so grateful that he told Groa that her warrior husband would soon be coming home. Overjoyed by the news, Groa forgot all her spells and was unable to further loosen the stone. After that, it was forbidden to cast a bone across the floor, for it was believed that such an action would stir the whetstone in Thor's poor head and cause him great pain.

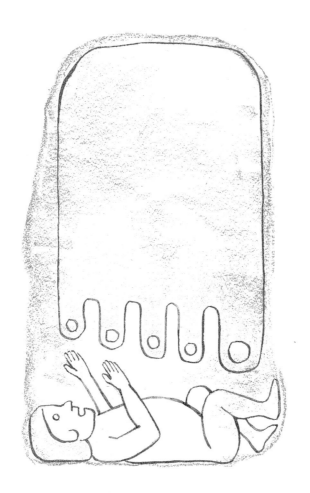

THIRTEEN

THE DEATH OF BALDER

Be not silent, Norn!
I will question thee
Until I know
Who will Balder's
Slayer be.

BALDER WAS THE MOST BEAUTIFUL of all the gods. He was so wise and kind and good that all heaven and earth adored him. Many considered him to be the light of the world.

But one night Balder had dark and terrible dreams. He dreamt that he was slain by an unknown enemy. In the morning he met with the gods in their council and told them about his dreams.

Everyone became frightened. They believed Balder's dark dreams were a warning that Balder would soon be harmed. "We must figure out how to protect my beloved son," said Odin.

Some recommended that Balder be guarded at all times. Others urged Odin to send him away. But Balder's mother, Frigg, had the best idea of all.

"I will go out in the nine worlds," the goddess said, "and secure a promise from all of nature that it will never bring harm to Balder."

The gods and goddesses applauded Frigg's plan, and she set out to make the world safe for her son.

Fire and water promised Frigg that they would never hurt Balder. Iron, metal, wood, stones, earth, disease, beasts, birds, and snakes — all assured Frigg that they would never bring harm to Balder.

Finally Frigg returned home, secure in the knowledge that her beloved son was safe.

The gods were so relieved that they played games, mocking fate. They shot arrows at Balder, only to watch their arrows miss their target. They threw stones at him, only to see their stones fall to the ground. They tried to stab Balder with their swords, but their swords bent in midair. They proved again and again that no harm could come to Balder.

All the gods celebrated Balder's invincible power, except for one. Loki, the trickster, grew jealous as he watched the gods at their play.

Loki's jealousy grew until he could bear it no longer. He disguised himself in woman's clothing and found Frigg in her palace.

When she saw Loki, Frigg mistook him for a servant-woman. "What is everyone doing outside?" she called from her spinning wheel. "Why are they laughing and clapping?"

"They're shooting arrows at Balder," said Loki in a high voice. "They're throwing stones at him to prove he cannot be harmed."

"Yes, of course," said Frigg. "That's because wood and stone promised me that they will never hurt him."

"Oh really?" said Loki. "So *all* of nature has promised not to harm your son?"

"Well, not quite all," said Frigg. "I did not bother with one small plant that grows on the eastern side of Valhalla — the mistletoe. It's too young and weak to ever hurt anyone."

"Ah, I see," said Loki. Smiling to himself, he slipped out of Frigg's hall and hurried into the woods east of Valhalla.

Loki searched the forest until he found a piece of mistletoe. He picked the sharp sprig, then rushed to the field where the gods were playing.

Hod, the blind twin of Balder, was standing outside the ring of players.

"Why do you not throw something at Balder?" asked Loki.

"Because I cannot see him," said Hod. "And because I have nothing to throw."

"Oh, but you must show honor to Balder the way the others do," said Loki. "I'll help you shoot him with this dart."

Loki placed the piece of mistletoe in Hod's hand. Then he directed Hod's aim and helped him send the mistletoe toward Balder.

The sharp sprig sailed through the air and lodged in Balder's heart. At once, Balder fell to the ground, dead.

The gods stared in disbelief at Balder's lifeless body. They knew that Loki had wrought this evil, but they could not take vengeance, for their pain and horror were too great.

None grieved more than Odin. With his deep wisdom and knowledge, he alone understood how disastrous was Balder's death. Odin knew that it meant that Ragnarok, the final battle of the world, was close at hand.

Frigg could not let go of her hope that Balder would return. She called the gods together and begged that one of them travel to the land of the dead to find her son and bring him back.

The god Hermod volunteered to go, and Odin gave him Sleipnir for his journey.

The grieving gods carried Balder's body down to the seashore to Balder's dragon-ship, *Ringhorn*.

The gods planned to make Balder's funeral pyre on *Ringhorn*. But when they tried to push the ship into the sea, it would not budge. They sent for a giantess named Hyrrokin, and she arrived on the back of a wolf, snapping reins made of twisted snakes.

Hyrrokin leaned against the ship's prow and with a single shove, she pushed *Ringhorn* into the water.

All the inhabitants of the nine worlds paraded in Balder's funeral procession. First came Odin and Frigg, the Valkyries, and Odin's two ravens. Then came Frey in his chariot drawn by the golden boar, and Freya in her chariot drawn by cats. Then came Thor, Sif, Nanna, Tyr, Heimdall, Bragi, Idun, Njord, Skadi, Gerd, and all the light elves, dark elves, and dwarves. Even the mountain-giants and frost-giants came down from their icy mountains and marched in Balder's funeral procession.

The gods carried Balder onto the ship. When his wife, Nanna, saw the body laid on the pyre, she died of a broken heart and was laid to rest beside her husband.

Odin placed his magic gold ring upon Balder's body, and the funeral pyre was set aflame. Then the burning ship was pushed out to sea.

Meanwhile, the god Hermod was proceeding on his mission to the land of the dead. On the back of Sleipnir, he galloped for nine days and nine nights through deep valleys filled with shadows. Finally he came to a glittering golden bridge.

"Stop! Who are you? Are you dead?" cried a maiden guarding the bridge.

"Not yet," said Hermod. "But I seek one who is — Balder, the fairest of the gods. Have you seen him by chance?"

"Yes," said the maiden. "He and his wife came over this bridge only yesterday. You'll find him if you follow the road to the north."

Hermod crossed the bridge, then traveled until he came to the barred gates of the land of the dead. He spurred Sleipnir, and the magic horse leapt into the air — sailing over the gates without even touching them.

Hermod rode on to the palace. When he entered Hel's home, he found Balder and Nanna sitting in the hall's most honored seats.

Hermod visited with his beloved brother all night. In the morning, he found Hel, the ruler of the dead, and begged her to let Balder and Nanna ride home with him. "The gods cannot stop mourning for this son of Odin," Hermod said.

Hearing these words, Hel's heart softened. "Return to the living," the monster said. "If you find that all beings weep for Balder, I will send him back to you. But if only one creature does not mourn this loss, I will keep him forever."

Before Hermod left, Balder placed Odin's magic ring in his hand. "Take this golden ring back to my father," Balder said. "Tell him I will see him soon."

"And please give this to Frigg," said Nanna, and she gave Hermod a beautiful woven rug.

Hermod said good-bye to Balder and Nanna. Then he rode night and day until he arrived back home.

When Hermod delivered the message from Hel, Odin and Frigg quickly sent messengers out from Asgard to bid the whole world to weep for the death of Balder. All creatures wept as they were asked: gods, goddesses, dwarves, light elves, dark elves, humans — even mountain-giants and frost-giants.

But as the messengers headed back to Asgard, convinced their mission had been successful, they came across a giantess sitting in a cave. She said her name was Thokk, though she was really Loki in disguise.

"Please weep for Balder," said a messenger. "The whole world must weep for him, so he can return from the land of the dead."

"Thokk will only weep with dry tears," Thokk said. "I loved him not. Let Hel keep him for as long as she likes."

And so Balder was not allowed to return to the land of the living. Thus the dark of winter was victorious over the light of the world.

TWILIGHT OF THE GODS

Axe-time, sword-time,
Shields are cloven.
Wind-time, wolf-time,
Ere the world falls.

LOKI WAS PUNISHED in the most dreadful way for Balder's death. He was bound to a rock, and a serpent was fastened above his head, its venom dripping onto his face. Loki's faithful wife, Sigyn, sat with him and tried to catch the poison in a basin. But every time she emptied the vessel, poison fell on Loki again, and the earth trembled as he writhed in pain.

When Loki finally broke free from his bondage, he turned completely against the gods and joined the forces of evil. Steering a ship over the seas, he sailed with the sons of Hel. Then, all of the monsters of the world joined them. The wolf Fenrir broke free from his fetters, the Midgard Serpent came from the sea, and the giants from the mountains. Together the evil force marched against Asgard.

Heimdall, the watchman, saw the army crossing the rainbow bridge. He grabbed the mighty trumpet that had never been sounded, and he gave it a long, deep blast.

The terrifying sound wakened all the gods. Odin put on his gold helmet, grabbed his magic spear, and led his warriors into battle.

The gods of Asgard met their foes on a huge plain. Odin attacked the wolf Fenrir. But the wolf devoured him.

Mighty Thor killed the Midgard Serpent, but then fell dead from the serpent's venom.

Frey battled the monster Hel, and lost.

Heimdall fought Loki, and each died by the hand of the other.

The eagle on top of the World Tree screamed with fear. The mighty tree trembled. Mountains crumbled. Seas flooded the land, and hot stars fell from the sky.

Brothers turned against brothers for greed's sake.

Terrible storms raged through the nine worlds.

The wolf Fenrir swallowed the sun, and Moon-Hound finally swallowed the moon. Flames engulfed heaven and earth and all the universe, and all things died — gods, goddesses, men, women, elves, dwarves, monsters, giants, birds, and beasts.

But after the nine worlds had been consumed by fire, the sun brought forth a daughter more lovely than herself. The earth began to turn green again. The eagle soared, and waterfalls flowed in the forests.

Miraculously, some of the gods returned to the world of the living — Balder and his blind twin Hod; and two sons of Thor, Modi and Magni. These gods met on the sunlit plain of Asgard, and they talked about time's morning. They remembered the Midgard Serpent, the wolf Fenrir, and the mighty Odin.

After they talked long and lovingly about the past, they returned to live in heaven, home of the wind.

During the terrible destruction of the universe, two humans had hidden themselves deep in a forest within the World Tree. They were named Life and Eager-for-Life. Now these two came out of hiding, and the dew of early morning served as their food.

From Life and Eager-for-Life came a great multitude of children who spread over the earth.

And thus began a new time and a new world.

MORE ABOUT THE NORSE MYTHS

WHERE DID THE NORSE MYTHS COME FROM?

THE NORSE MYTHS CAME from a group of people called the Vikings, who included Danish people, Norwegians, and Swedes. The word "Vikings" means "fighting men," or "settling men." The age of the Vikings was the period 780 to 1070. During that time, the Vikings attacked villages in Britain, France, Germany, and Spain. The Vikings from Norway sailed to Greenland, Iceland, and even North America. They traveled to Iceland in 840, and many Viking families settled there and lived on farms. At first, they still believed in the old Norse gods and goddesses, but all of them converted to Christianity in the year 1000. Thereafter, fragments of the old stories and myths were written down in two manuscripts called the *Poetic (Elder) Edda* and the *Prose (Younger) Edda*.

Today our main sources of Norse mythology are the *Poetic Edda* and the *Prose Edda*. They provide us with nearly all the stories that make up the Norse myths. The *Poetic Edda* contains thirty-four poems composed over a thousand years ago by different poets who believed in the old gods. Then later they were compiled by an unknown person or persons. Some believe the person might have been a scholar named Saemunder, but this cannot be proven.

The *Prose Edda* was written by Snorri Sturluson, an Icelandic chieftain and poet who lived eight hundred years ago. Sturluson wrote a number of myths and tales, some of which are retellings of the poems in the *Poetic Edda*.

GODS AND GODDESSES

BALDER (BAHL-der) was the son of Odin and Frigg. He was the most gentle and beautiful of the gods. All the world grieved when he was unwittingly slain by his twin brother Hod, who was tricked by Loki.

BOR (BOHR) was the son of Buri, the first god. Bor had three sons: Odin, Vili, and Ve.

BRAGI (BRAH-gee) was one of Odin's sons. He was god of poetry and the husband of Idun, the keeper of the golden apples of youth.

BURI (BU-ree) was licked into being by the cow Audumla. Though called a giant, he was the grandfather of Odin and forefather of all the gods and goddesses.

FJORGYN (FYOOR-gen) was the mother of Thor by Odin. She was an earth goddess.

FREY (FRAY) was one of the Vanir, the gods of fertility. Son of Njord and brother of Freya, he was the god of rain and harvests.

FREYA (FRAY-ah) was a fertility goddess. She drove a chariot pulled by cats and had a magic falcon suit. She was the daughter of Njord and the sister of Frey.

FRIGG (FRIG) was Odin's wife and the mother of Balder and Hod. She knew the future, but kept all that she knew to herself.

HEIMDALL (HAME-dahl) was a son of Odin and the guardian of the gods. He blew his trumpet to signal the end of the world.

HERMOD (HEHR-mood) was the son of Odin who rode to the land of the dead to bring Balder and Nanna back.

HOD (HAWD) was the blind son of Odin and Frigg who unwittingly killed his twin brother, Balder.

IDUN (EE-doon) was the keeper of the golden apples of youth. She was married to the god Bragi.

LOKI (LOH-kee) was actually a giant, as he was the son of two giants. But a blood brother to Odin, he lived in Asgard as one of the gods. Loki was a trickster and mischief-maker and brought about the end of the world.

MAGNI (MAHG-nee) was the young son of Thor who miraculously lifted a giant's foot off his father's neck.

MIMIR (MEE-meer) was a god who possessed great wisdom. Though his head was severed from his body, he continued to live and guarded Mimir's Well, whose waters were the source of great wisdom and memory.

NANNA (NAH-nah) was Balder's loyal wife. After Balder's death, she died of grief, then traveled with him to the land of the dead.

NJORD (NYOOR) was a Vanir god, or a god of fertility. He was the father of Frey and Freya. Ruler of the seas and the wind, he married the giantess Skadi.

NORNS (NORNZ) were three maidens who could forecast the future. They determined at the birth of every god and human whether or not the individual would have a good life or bad life. Their names were Urd, which means "fate"; Skuld, which means "being"; and Verdandi, which means "necessity."

ODIN (O-din) was the greatest of all the gods. He was known as the god of war and death, the master magician, the god of poetry, and lord of the runes. He presided over Valhalla, the Hall of the Slain. Any warrior who died in battle became Odin's son and feasted with him in Valhalla. Odin was the husband of Frigg and father of Bragi, Thor, Hermod, Heimdall, Hod, and Balder.

SIF (SEEF) was the wife of Thor. She had beautiful golden hair which gleamed like ripe corn.

SIGYN (SEH-gen) was the faithful wife of Loki. She tried to ease his terrible agony when he was punished by the gods.

SKIRNIR (SKEER-neer) was the messenger of the god Frey. He helped Frey win the giantess Gerd for his bride.

THIALFI (thee-ALF-fee) was the young servant of Thor who traveled with him to the fortress of Utgard.

THOR (THOR) was the son of Odin and husband of Sif. Strongest of all the gods, he wielded a mighty hammer and was known as the god of thunder.

TYR (TEER) was the god who sacrificed his hand to the wolf Fenrir. In old Norse literature, he was called the god of war; he was sometimes depicted as the son of Odin, but at other times as the son of the giant Hymir.

VALKYRIES (VAHL-kure-reez) were warrior goddesses who rode across the sky to the battlefields. They picked up the slain warriors and carried them back to Valhalla, Odin's Hall of the Slain.

VANIR (VAH-neer) were the nature gods, or fertility gods who fought the Aesir. When a truce was called, three Vanir — Njord, Frey, and Freya — went to live in Asgard.

NOTE: Every day we use words that are derived from the names of Norse gods and goddesses. For example, the word *Tuesday* comes from "Tyr's-day." *Wednesday* comes from "Woden's-day." ("Woden" is Odin's name in German.) *Thursday* comes from "Thor's-day," and *Friday*, from "Freya's-day."

GIANTS, GIANTESSES, DWARVES

BROK (BROK) was the brother of the dwarf Sindri, who gave Thor his hammer.

GERD (GAIRD) was a beautiful frost-giantess who at first refused to marry the god Frey.

GUNLOD (GUNE-lawd) was the daughter of the giant Suttung. Guardian of the Mead of Poetry, she gave the precious drink to Odin.

HRUNGNIR (HROONG-neer) was the strongest of the giants. Before he was slain by Thor, he tried to fool the thunder god by hiding behind a clay giant.

HYMIR (HEE-meer) was a giant who owned the enormous cauldron desired by Thor. Father of the god Tyr, he lived at the border of heaven.

HYRROKIN (HEE-rawk-keen) was a giantess who dragged Balder's boat, *Ringhorn*, down to sea.

IVALDI (ee-VAHL-dee) was father of the two dwarves who gave three treasures to the gods.

LOGI (LOH-gee) was a giant who beat Loki in an eating contest at the fortress of Utgard.

SKADI (SKAH-dee) was the daughter of the giant Thiazi. Judging the gods by looking only at their feet, she chose the sea god, Njord, to be her husband.

SINDRI (SIN-dree) was a dwarf who gave three wondrous gifts to the gods, including Thor's hammer.

SKRYMIR (SKREE-meer) was a trickster giant who crossed paths with Thor on his way to the fortress of Utgard.

SUTTUNG (SOOT-tung) was a giant who refused to give the Mead of Poetry to the gods.

THIAZI (thee-AH-zee) was a giant who disguised himself as an eagle and stole the golden apples of youth from the gods. Later his daughter, Skadi, sought to avenge his death.

THOKK (THOCK) was a giantess who was actually Loki in disguise. She refused to weep for Balder, therefore not allowing him to leave the land of the dead.

THRYM (THRIM) was a giant who stole Thor's hammer, and would only return it on the condition that the goddess Freya marry him.

YMIR (EE-meer) was the first frost-giant. He was formed out of ice and fire. Later the gods used his body to make the universe.

CREATURES

AUDUMLA (OUD-hoom-la) was a great cow created out of the icy void. By licking the ice, she licked Buri, forefather of all the gods, into being.

FENRIR (FEN-reer) was one of Loki's three monstrous children. He was a fierce wolf. He was bound by the gods until the end of the universe, when he broke free from his fetters and fought Odin to the death.

GOLDFAX (GOLD-fax), which means "Gold Mane," was the horse that belonged to the giant Hrungnir. After Thor slew Hrungnir, he gave Goldfax to Thor's young son Magni.

HEL (HEL) was the hideous offspring of Loki who ruled the realm of the dead.

MIDGARD SERPENT (MEED-gahrd SER-pent) was another of Loki's three monstrous children. It lived in the sea, its body encircling all of Midgard.

RATATOSK (RAH-tah-tosk) was a squirrel who carried insults back and forth between the eagle at the top of the World Tree and the serpent, who lived under the base of the tree.

SLEIPNIR (SLEP-neer) was Odin's powerful eight-legged horse. The fastest steed in the nine worlds, he could fly over land and sea.

THE NINE WORLDS

ALFHEIM (AHLF-hame) was the world of the light elves.

ASGARD (AHZ-gahrd) was the world of the Aesir gods and goddesses.

JOTUNHEIM (YOH-tun-hame) was the world of the frost-giants.

MUSPELL (MOOS-pel) was the world of fire.

NIFLHEIM (NIFF-el-hame) was the world of mist and the dead.

NIDAVELLIR (NEED-ah-vel-eer) was the world of the dwarves.

MIDGARD (MEED-gahrd) was the world of humans.

SVARTALFHEIM (svart-ALF-hame) was the world of the dark elves.

VANAHEIM (VAH-nah-hame) was the world of the Vanir gods.

SPECIAL THINGS, EVENTS, AND PLACES

BIFROST (BEE-frost) was the rainbow bridge, which connected the world of humans to the world of the gods.

GINNUNGAGAP (GIN-noon-gah-GAHP) was the great void between Muspell and Niflheim before the creation of the nine worlds.

RAGNAROK (RAHG-nah-rock) was the final battle, which destroyed all the nine worlds.

RINGHORN (RING-horn) was Balder's funeral ship. It was the biggest ship in the world.

RUNES (ROONZ) were mysterious written symbols, which gave Odin magic power over nature.

THRYMHEIM (THRIM-hame) was the hall of the giant Thrym.

UTGARD (OOT-gahrd) was a fortress in the land of the giants.

VALHALLA (vahl-HAHL-lah) was Odin's Hall of the Slain. All day the armored heroes fought one another in the courtyard; and all night they drank and feasted together. Set in a grove of trees in Asgard, Valhalla had walls made of spears and a roof thatched with shields. Each day, eight hundred heroes came and went through Valhalla's five-hundred-and-forty doors.

YGGDRASILL (EGG-drah-sil) was the World Tree, which sheltered the nine worlds.

SYMBOLS

NORSE MYTHOLOGY IS FILLED with *symbols*, or images that represent other things. For instance, the giants of Norse myths represent the wild forces of nature. Sif's golden hair represents the golden wheat harvests. The giantess Gerd symbolizes icy, wintry weather. The god Frey symbolizes the warmth and gentleness of the spring rains. The two ravens that sit on Odin's shoulders symbolize thought and memory. Thor's hammer represents law and order. The trickster Loki symbolizes fire — both its good and bad aspects.

The number nine is also an important symbol in Norse mythology. Nine worlds are encompassed by the World Tree. Odin hangs on a tree for nine nights in order to learn the magic runes; he kills nine trolls to help win the Mead of Poetry. The god Hermod travels for nine days and nights to the land of the dead. The number nine often symbolizes death and rebirth in different mythologies. Perhaps this is because it ends the series of single numbers.

These are but a few examples of the rich symbolism in Norse mythology.

RUNES

RUNES ARE WRITTEN SYMBOLS of a primitive alphabet, created by early Germanic and Scandinavian tribes in Europe. "Rune" comes from a Gothic word meaning "secret," as few people understood the mysterious symbols. They were used as charms and healing formulas and were carved upon drinking horns, weapons, and stones. Though the runes were used mainly for magical purposes, some scholars believe they were also used for legal documents, family histories, and poems. After the Germanic peoples became Christian, the runic letters were eventually replaced by the Roman alphabet.

BIBLIOGRAPHY

ANDERSON, RASMUS B., *Norse Mythology*, Chicago: Scott, Foresman and Co., 1901.

BELLOWS, HENRY ADAMS (translator), *The Poetic Edda*, London: American-Scandanavian Foundation, 1923.

BRAY, OLIVE (translator), *The Poetic Edda*, London: AMS Press, 1908.

BRODEUR, ARTHUR GILCHRIST (translator), *The Prose Edda*, by Snorri Sturluson, London: American-Scandinavian Foundation, 1923.

CROSSLEY-HOLLAND, KEVIN, *The Norse Myths*, New York: Pantheon Books, 1980.

D'AULAIRE, INGRI AND EDGAR PARIN, *Norse Gods and Giants*, New York: Doubleday and Co., 1967.

DAVIDSON, H. R. ELLIS, *Gods and Myths of Northern Europe*, Middlesex, England: Penguin Books Ltd., 1964.

EDMISON, JOHN P., *Stories from the Norseland*, Philadelphia: Penn Publishing Co., 1909.

GUERBER, H.A., *The Norsemen*, London: Studio Editions, 1993.

HAMILTON, EDITH, *Mythology*, Boston: Little Brown & Co., 1940.

HOLLANDER, LEE M. (translator), *The Poetic Edda*, Austin: University of Texas Press, 1929.

HOSFORD, DOROTHY, *Thunder of the Gods*, New York: Holt, Rinehart and Winston, 1952.

PICARD, BARBARA LEONIE, *Tales of the Norse Gods and Heroes*, Oxford: Oxford University Press, 1953.

A NOTE ABOUT THE ART

THE VIKINGS LEFT BEHIND many crude, simplistic images carved in stone, bone, and wood. They have been found throughout Scandinavia and in other regions of the Viking world, which once extended as far west as North America and as far east as the Caspian Sea. With this type of art, the Norse people told their stories and recorded their deeds. Many of Mr. Howell's ideas for his compositions came from that early Viking art. His intention for this book was to make ancient art come vividly to life.

To do this, the artist first created primitive-style drawings, based on Viking art, to open each chapter. He then created a dramatic realization of those images in his full-page paintings. If you look closely at the paintings, you will find the same primitive version scratched onto its surface. In this way, Mr. Howell transforms his ancient images into dramatic, realistic scenes before the readers' eyes.

INDEX